HIP-HOP STARS

TUPAC SHAKUR

HIP-HOP STARS

Sean Combs
Eminem
Jay-Z
Queen Latifah
Tupac Shakur

HIP-HOP STARS

TUPAC SHAKUR

Clifford W. Mills

Checkmark Books®
An imprint of Infobase Publishing

TUPAC SHAKUR

Checkmark Books
An imprint of Infobase Publishing
132 West 31st Street
New York, NY 10001

Library of Congress Cataloging-in-Publication Data

Mills, Cliff, 1947-
  Tupac Shakur / Clifford W. Mills.
    p. cm. — (Hip-hop stars)
  Includes bibliographical references and index.
  ISBN 978-0-7910-9495-2 (hardcover) — ISBN 978-0-7910-9732-8 (pbk.) 1. Shakur, Tupac, 1971–1996—Juvenile literature. 2. Rap musicians—United States—Biography—Juvenile literature. I. Title. II. Series.

  ML3930.S48M55 2007
  782.421649092—dc22
  [B]
                        2007020898

Checkmark Books are available at special discounts when purchased in bulk quantities for businesses, associations, institutions, or sales promotions. Please call our Special Sales Department in New York at (212) 967-8800 or (800) 322-8755.

You can find Chelsea House on the World Wide Web at http://www.chelseahouse.com

Text design by Erik Lindstrom
Cover design by Ben Peterson

Printed in the United States of America

Bang NMSG 10 9 8 7 6 5 4 3 2 1

This book is printed on acid-free paper.

All links and Web addresses were checked and verified to be correct at the time of publication. Because of the dynamic nature of the Web, some addresses and links may have changed since publication and may no longer be valid.

CONTENTS

INTRODUCTION
By Chuck D

Hip-Hop: A Brief History

Like the air we breathe, hip-hop seems to be everywhere. The lifestyle that many thought would be a passing fad has, three decades later, grown to become a permanent part of world culture. Hip-hop artists have become some of today's heroes, replacing the comic book worship of decades past and joining athletes and movie stars as the people kids dream of being. Names like 50 Cent, P. Diddy, Russell Simmons, Jay-Z, Foxy Brown, Snoop Dogg, and Flavor Flav now ring as familiar as Elvis, Babe Ruth, Marilyn Monroe, and Charlie Chaplin.

While the general public knows many of the names, videos, and songs branded by the big companies that make them popular, it's also important to know the holy trinity, the founding fathers of hip-hop: Kool DJ Herc, Grandmaster Flash, and

Afrika Bambaataa. All are deejays who played and presented the records that rappers and dancers delighted themselves upon. Bambaataa single-handedly stopped the gang wars in the 1970s with the themes of peace, unity, love, and having fun.

Hip-hop is simply a term for a form of artistic creativity that was spawned in New York City—more precisely the Bronx—in the early to mid-1970s. Amid the urban decay in the areas where black and Hispanic people dwelled, economic, educational, and environmental resources were depleted. Jobs and businesses were all but moved away. Living conditions were of a lower standard than the rest of the city and country. Last but not least, art and sports programs in the schools were the first to be cut for the sake of lowering budgets; thus, music classes, teaching the subject's history and techniques, were all but lost.

From these ashes, like a phoenix, rose an art form. Through the love of technology and records found in family collections or even those tossed out on the street, the deejay emerged. Different from the ones heard on the radio, these folk were innovating a style that was popular on the island of Jamaica. Two turntables kept the music continuous, with the occasional voice on top of the records. This was the very humble beginning of rap music.

Rap music is actually two distinct words: rap and music. "Rap" is the vocal application that is used on top of the music. On a vocal spectrum, it is between talking and singing and is one of the few alternatives for vocalizing to emerge in the last 50 years. It's important to know that inventors and artists are side by side in the importance of music's development. Let's remember that inventor Thomas A. Edison created the first recording with "Mary Had a Little Lamb" in 1878, most likely in New Jersey, the same state where the first rap recording—Sugarhill Gang's "Rapper's Delight"—was made more than 100 years later, in 1979.

It's hard to separate the importance of history, science, language arts, and education when discussing music. Because of the social silencing of black people in the United States from slavery in the 1600s to civil rights in the 1960s, much sentiment, dialogue, and soul is wrapped within the cultural expression of music. In eighteenth-century New Orleans, slaves gathered on Sundays in Congo Square to socialize and play music. Within this captivity, many dialects, customs, and styles combined with instrumentation, vocals, and rhythm to form a musical signal or code of preservation. These are the foundations of jazz and the blues. Likewise, it's impossible to separate hip-hop and rap music from the creativity of the past. Look within the expression and words of black music and you'll get a reflection of history itself. The four creative elements of hip-hop—emceeing (the art of vocalization); deejaying (the musician-like manipulation of records); break dancing (the body expression of the music); and graffiti (the drawn graphic expression of the culture)—have been intertwined in the community before and since slavery.

However, just because these expressions were introduced by the black-Hispanic underclass, doesn't mean that others cannot create or appreciate hip-hop. Hip-hop is a cultural language used best to unite the human family all around the world. To peep the global explosion, one need not search far. Starting just north of the U.S. border, Canadian hip-hop has featured indigenous rappers who are infusing different language and dialect flows into their work, from Alaskan Eskimo to French flowing cats from Montreal and the rest of Quebec's provincial region. Few know that France for many years has been the second largest hip-hop nation, measured not just by high sales numbers, but also by a very political philosophy. Hip-hop has been alive and present since the mid-1980s in Japan and other Asian countries. Australia has been a hotbed in welcoming world rap acts, and it has also created its own vibrant hip-hop scene, with the reminder of its government's takeover of indigenous people reflected in every rapper's flow and rhyme. As a rhythm of the people, the continents of Africa and South America (especially Ghana, Senegal, and South Africa, Brazil, Surinam, and Argentina) have long mixed traditional homage into the new beats and rhyme of this millennium.

Hip-hop has been used to help Brazilian kids learn English when school systems failed to bridge the difficult language gap of Portuguese and patois to American English. It has entertained and enlightened youth, and has engaged political discussion in society, continuing the tradition of the African griots (storytellers) and folk singers.

For the past 25 years, hip-hop has been bought, sold, followed, loved, hated, praised, and blamed. History has shown that other cultural music forms in the United States have been just as misunderstood and held under public scrutiny. The history of the people who originated the art form can be found in the music itself. The timeline of recorded rap music spans more than a quarter century, and that is history in itself.

Presidents, kings, queens, fame, famine, infamy, from the great wall of China to the Berlin wall, food, drugs, cars, hate, and love have been rhymed and scratched. This gives plenty reason for social study. And I don't know what can be more fun than learning the history of something so relevant to young minds and souls as music.

A Warrior Poet Is Born

Our world has always had warrior poets. They are special people who have lived in almost every society, from ancient Greece to modern Asia and America. The Irish had secret societies of men and women who were professional protectors of the poor and voiceless, and also were gifted storytellers. Some ancient Greek, Aztec, and Inca warriors were proud of being both fearless in battle and poets when the battles were over. Medieval knights often were both skillful fighters and accomplished poets and musicians. Eighteenth-century Asian martial artists walked the earth righting wrongs and dispensing wisdom in equal measures. They were respected, feared, and inspired.

Warrior poets have double natures. They are physically strong but care about the weak. They are combative but don't fight their emotions. They are tough when they need to be, but only when they need to be. They are proud of who they are but fearless about who they want to become. They experience horror and tragedy but rise above them with poetry and song. Hip-hop legend Tupac Amaru Shakur was a warrior poet. This is his story.

Warrior poets in history and legend often have special births and special gifts. Tupac Shakur had both. His story begins in the middle of a turbulent time in American history and with his mother.

ALICE DOESN'T LIVE HERE

Alice Faye Williams was born in 1947 and lived her early years in Lumberton, North Carolina. Lumberton is a small city tucked into the coastal plains of the southeastern part of the state, famous for its trees and lumber. It was, like much of the American South in the 1940s, a segregated city. Alice was a tomboy, active and athletic, but even as a young child she knew she wanted to experience more of the world.

When she moved to New York City at age 11, she changed. She felt the restless energy of the city and decided she wanted to become an actor. She applied to the High School for the Performing Arts (made famous by the movie *Fame*) when she was in ninth grade and was accepted after an exhausting audition. At school, she was a creative and smart student in drama, dance, and writing. She was forceful in everything she did.

But, she was also poor. She did not arrive in a limousine as some kids did, nor did she have beautiful clothes that called attention to her. She could barely afford the required leotards. She was short on bus fare most days and sometimes had to ask neighbors for their spare change. The school had no cafeteria, so at lunchtime most of the students went to Times Square to hang out and eat. Alice couldn't afford to go

In his short life, Tupac Shakur made an indelible impression on the world. A sensitive artist and commercial success, Tupac was also caught up in the violent drama of gangsta rap's East Coast–West Coast rivalry. His immense talent and promise were cut short by petty feuding, and as a result, he has become a cultural icon along the lines of James Dean, Marilyn Monroe, and Kurt Cobain. More than a decade after his death, Tupac has become the best-selling rap artist in the world.

with them. She began to feel like she lived in a world apart from most of her schoolmates. She didn't like the feeling—in fact, she hated it.

Alice started skipping afternoon classes and sharing some Thunderbird wine with some of the people in the neighborhood. She tried to dull the pain of feeling poor and inadequate. By her junior year, she had dropped out of school, disappointing herself and those who cared for her. She was starting to abuse alcohol, but it couldn't numb the anger of being young and different and poor.

A WOMAN CHANGED

One day at Manny's Bar on 169th Street in the Bronx, Alice met a man who turned her on to the teachings of Malcolm X and the Nation of Islam. Malcolm X was a man of many messages, but he is perhaps best known for teaching African Americans to unite and feel pride in their heritage and identity. He also encouraged African Americans to fight back however they could against racist Americans and a capitalist economic system that built in inequality by favoring those who started with money and trapping those who didn't. The 1960s were in full swing, and the country was changing. Those changes were hitting fast and forcefully right in New York City.

Alice began to absorb the lessons of Malcolm X, of knowing who she was, what her heritage was, and what she could do to support herself. She cut her hair into a natural style, began to wear African-inspired clothing, and changed her name. She became Afeni, which means "lover of people." Her last name became Shakur, which is Arabic for "thankful to God," when she married Lumumba Shakur, another convert to the teachings of Malcolm X. African Americans were well aware that their family names had been given to their ancestors by slave masters, and many were choosing their "real" names for themselves. Cassius Clay and Lew Alcindor had become Muhammad Ali and Kareem Abdul Jabbar respectively. These were not just

The lessons of Malcolm X *(above)* inspired countless people, especially young African Americans in the 1960s. Tupac Shakur's mother, Afeni, was one of them, and she taught those values to her son.

name changes. They were personal transformations and assertions of liberty.

Afeni Shakur had gotten a job in the U.S. government, one of only two women accepted to become mail carriers

MALCOLM X

Malcolm X was a man whose words inspired both admiration and fear, depending on the listener. If Martin Luther King Jr. became the spokesperson for nonviolent approaches to advancing civil rights, Malcolm X was the spokesperson for more direct and even violent action to combat racism.

Malcolm Little grew up in extremes, with a preacher for a father and a mother who had been threatened by the Ku Klux Klan when she was pregnant with him. He knew racial hatred from the inside. After dropping out of school at 15 and getting caught up in drug dealing, gambling, and robbery, he served a long prison term. He gave himself a higher education in the prison library—including learning about the Nation of Islam, a religious organization headed by Elijah Muhammad.

After leaving prison, he changed his name to Malcolm "X" to show that "Little" was a last name given to his ancestors by slave owners. He soon became the second most important leader of the Nation of Islam, after Elijah Muhammad, and many think a rivalry for power between the two intensified as Malcolm X became more famous through his speeches and writing.

In March 1964, Malcolm withdrew from the Nation of Islam and started his own organization, the Moslem Mosque. He advocated political and economic black nationalism, not just religious nationalism, and soon converted to orthodox Islam. Malcolm preached that black people should only be nonviolent with those

in the New York area. Part of her route was in downtown Manhattan, on Wall Street. Afeni saw close-up the reality that there were the haves and have nots, and the haves had a lot. Her creativity and talent were redirected into becoming more

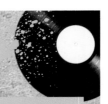

who were nonviolent to them—blacks should treat others as they themselves were being treated.

Malcolm began collaborating with author Alex Haley on a book to be called *The Autobiography of Malcolm X*. When it was published in 1965, *Time* magazine hailed it as one of the ten most important nonfiction books of the twentieth century. In the autobiography, he says that a religious pilgrimage to Mecca in 1964 transformed him from a hater of white people to someone who simply doesn't believe in any form of discrimination:

> My pilgrimage broadened my scope. It blessed me with new insight. In two weeks in the Holy Land, I saw what I had never seen in thirty-nine years here in America. I saw all races, all colors—blue-eyed blonds to black-skinned Africans—in true brotherhood! . . . No segregationists—no liberals; they would not have known the meaning of those words. In the past, yes, I have made sweeping indictments of all white people. I will never be guilty of that again.

On February 21, 1965, Malcolm was giving a speech in New York when he was assassinated by three men using handguns and a shotgun. There are those who believe the murder was planned and executed by Elijah Muhammad sympathizers, but that has never been proven.

active politically. The civil rights movement had by then built into an unstoppable force, starting with the famous Freedom Riders in 1961, but the movement had many forces within it, not all pulling in the same direction. One of the forces was the Black Panthers, one of the most militant civil rights organizations in the country. The Black Panthers had started in Oakland, California, and had quickly become famous for its confrontations with authorities. When Afeni heard Black Panther cofounder Bobby Seale speak at a rally in Harlem, she thought she had heard "revolutionary poetry." Seale called for better schools, better housing, and better protection for black people in the United States. He preached the need for self-defense, using legal means when possible, and shotguns when the law failed. Afeni recalled later in her autobiography, *Evolution of a Revolutionary,* that "He could recruit a town full of black people" when he spoke of the Panther program. She thought now that as a woman of color at this time in America she was going to have to fight for her political and economic rights and not assume they would be given to her. She and others would get hurt, but wars come in many sizes and shapes, and she was now in a war. She joined the growing army of Black Panthers.

"ONE BLACK WOMAN"

With her extraordinary energy and brains, Afeni quickly rose to the top of the New York chapter of the Black Panthers. Her husband, Lumumba Shakur, and she became targets of suspicion by police and FBI forces alarmed at the threatening and confrontational styles of the Panthers. On April 2, 1969, Afeni and her husband were arrested in their Harlem apartment and charged with conspiracy and weapons possession. She was sent to jail from April 1969 to January 1970 to await trial but then was released on bail. She threw herself into the fight for her life by organizing fund-raising events for the jailed Panthers and rallying support for their cause. In the middle of this

Bobby Seale *(above)* **cofounded the Black Panther party with Huey Newton. Inspired by the words of Malcolm X, Seale broke from the generally nonviolent Civil Rights Movement to create the Black Panthers, a militant group fighting for black empowerment.**

political storm, she found brief comfort with a man named Billy Garland and became pregnant. She did not think she could conceive, so she was startled.

Afeni was sent back to prison in the New York Women's House of Detention, and she had to sue prison officials to get an egg and a glass of milk a day so her unborn child could be nourished. Already, she was fighting for her son.

She acted as her own lawyer in the trial on the conspiracy and weapons charges. People thought she was crazy to do so. In her cell, she prepared a summary argument that was described as "brilliant" by those who heard it in court. She later said in her autobiography that she thought this would be the last time she would be able to speak before spending the rest of her life in jail: "I was young, I was arrogant . . . I wouldn't have been able to be brilliant if I thought I was going to get out of jail . . . I had to make a record there for later, because I would never be able to speak again." On May 13, 1971, Afeni and the other Black Panthers on trial with her (collectively called the New York Panther 21) were found not guilty. Her brilliance had saved her.

COMING INTO LIFE

Only a few weeks after being set free, Afeni gave birth to her baby boy, her "prince," on June 16, 1971. She first called him Lesane Parish Crooks (some sources say Parish Lesane Crooks), but soon gave him the name Tupac Amaru, after a revolutionary Incan leader who had fought the Spanish conquistadors. The name means "shining serpent, blessed one." Her son later said he thought the name meant "intelligent warrior." She wanted him to know that he was a citizen of the world, not just of a neighborhood in New York.

Tupac Amaru Shakur later said in a book and movie named *Tupac: Resurrection* that "When I was born there was a moment of calm peace, then the three minutes after that, it was on." The sounds of prison were now replaced by the sounds of Roberta Flack's "That's No Way to Say Goodbye" as Afeni and her sister Glo watched over the active and thrashing baby and tried to get him to sleep. It was usually a losing battle.

They all lived in Greenwich Village, in lower Manhattan, and then in East Harlem, in upper New York City, both sources of sights and sounds unlike those seen in most of the country but often experienced in some of the wider world. Afeni wanted to expose Tupac to music and culture at a very early age, and one of the first live-music performances he

Afeni and Lumumba Shakur *(center and right)* **are escorted from a New York City police station on April 3, 1969. The Shakurs were arrested for their connection with a Black Panther plot to bomb five Manhattan department stores. With this incarceration, Tupac got his first taste of prison life from inside the womb.**

heard was Gil Scott-Heron and the Midnight Band at the legendary Village Vanguard. Scott-Heron was a jazz vocalist famous for his song "The Revolution Will Not Be Televised." Tupac seemed almost hypnotized by the sounds and looked like he wanted to be on the stage performing as well.

Afeni and Aunt Glo made wonderful dishes of curried shrimp, fish, and fried chicken, and the whole family remembers going to the Columbus Avenue International Food Fair with its African, Indian, and Japanese dishes. Tupac Amaru was indeed a citizen of the world. He could hear African drummers, jazz musicians, and poets in his own living room, either from Afeni's extensive record collection or live from her friends. Family celebrations were usually with extended family, drawn from Glo's children, women in the Black Panthers, neighbors, and friends.

By 1973, Afeni was no longer with her husband Lumumba. She had fallen into a relationship with and later married Mutulu Shakur (no relation to Lumumba), an acupuncturist and a Black Panther as well. She soon gave birth to Tupac's only sibling, Sekyiwa, when Tupac was two. Mutulu had a son, Mopreme, who had become Tupac's older stepbrother.

Afeni had become a paralegal for South Bronx Legal Services to lead fights against police brutality, expose injustices in the legal system, and organize renters who were having their rights trampled on. She was still at war, but her battles were more carefully chosen, and she had more legal weapons to use. The 1960s had given way to the 1970s, and political confrontations had changed ever since the killing of two Black Panthers in their beds in late 1969 and the killing of four Kent State University student protesters by the Ohio National Guard in May 1970. The country had recoiled in shock with such a horrible display of Americans killing Americans.

A FULL EDUCATION

Jamal Joseph, Tupac's brilliant biographer and family friend, wrote in *Tupac Shakur Legacy* about this period in Tupac's life:

> If Tupac misbehaved, Afeni sat down and talked to him as well as issuing any discipline. "What would an independent black man do?" she began asking him as early as age two. "I wanted him to think and live as an independent black man." To punish him for things like teasing his sister or pulling

a prank, Afeni would make Tupac read from the *New York Times* and give a full explanation of what he had just read. She worked writing into his discipline, having him think about what he had done, and why, and put it down on paper. . . . "I encouraged him to write out his thoughts and emotions," Afeni said. "Not the things he thought I wanted to hear but the things he was really feeling."

Afeni later told Joseph and others that she knew she was raising a young black man in a hostile society, and that his best weapon for self-defense would be a "strong, brilliant, and agile mind." Once Tupac ran after a ball and fell on the sidewalk, cutting his forehead badly. Emergency room doctors started to put restraints on him before they stitched his head, standard procedure then for treating an active young child. Afeni told the doctors not to tie her son down like a criminal but rather explain to him what they were doing. They did and even gave him a mirror to watch. He watched calmly as the doctors stitched up his wound.

Afeni was not alone in raising her son. Mutulu Shakur, his stepfather, took him to martial arts classes and to an acupuncture clinic Mutulu owned, where Tupac saw him treat a wide range of people, including drug addicts. Glo's husband, Tom Cox (known as T.C.), was a father figure, teaching him to work hard and value his family. One of the Black Panthers, Elmer "Geronimo" Pratt, was on trial for conspiracy and murder, and Afeni was head of his defense committee. She took Tupac to meet with Pratt several times, and Tupac later said he considered Pratt his godfather. Pratt was a strong and no-nonsense Black Panther leader, and he was a figure of towering strength to many around him; he was the "Minister of Defense" for the Panthers. Tupac learned well from his "fathers" and from his mother that he had to protect his baby sister, his stepbrother, and his cousins. He could pick on them, but everyone else in the neighborhood learned not to.

Part of Tupac's intense and varied education included religion. Afeni and her children went to services led by Reverend Herbert Daugherty at the House of Lord Church in Brooklyn. When Reverend Daugherty asked Tupac what he wanted to be when he grew up, Tupac famously replied, "a revolutionary."

Tupac inherited his mother's talent for and love of performing, and even at a very young age he wrote, directed, and acted in his own plays and skits. He especially loved to imitate martial arts expert Bruce Lee. That was his warrior side. But he also loved to read, write in his journal, and create rhymes with his friends. That was his poet side. Soon, Tupac spoke and performed at many political events and rallies, including giving a speech at a rally in support of Geronimo Pratt in front of Harlem's New York State Office Building.

Afeni enrolled her son in creative-arts workshops that included dance, writing, and music. She brought him to a Harlem theater company known as the 127th Street Ensemble, and Tupac so impressed its director that he became a member at age eleven. After only a year, he got the role of Travis in Lorraine Hansberry's *A Raisin in the Sun*. Tupac loved the role and performing—it gave him a real and natural high. Activist and presidential candidate Reverend Jesse Jackson was one of the members of the audience. Their paths would cross again.

Like many children, Tupac watched a lot of television. When he was very young, his mother was away on business a good deal of time. He fought loneliness just as many kids do. In *Tupac: Resurrection* he described some of his early life:

> When I was young I was quiet, withdrawn. I read a lot, wrote poetry, kept a diary. I watched TV . . . It was when I was in front of the TV by myself, being alone in the house by myself, having to cook dinner by myself, eat by myself . . . I thought if I could be and act like those characters [on TV], act like those people, I could have some of their joy. If I could act like I had a big family I wouldn't feel as lonely.

Elmer "Geronimo" Pratt *(above)*, leader of the Los Angeles chapter of the Black Panthers, awaits a verdict on his six-month-long trial, on December 15, 1971. Pratt was charged with conspiracy to kill police, and Afeni Shakur was head of his defense committee.

Even though he was often alone, he later looked back on the years in New York as some of the happiest times of his life. Tupac remembered his strong and loving mother's world of culture and opportunity and the close relationships with father figures and relatives as a good way to grow up. He also said he missed having a real father, however. Later, he would try to fill that void in many ways.

A warrior poet had been born and bred, and now he needed to walk the earth. He would be in danger for the rest of his life. But he would also bring art to his world and ours.

A Broken World

In 1984, when Tupac was thirteen, Afeni lost her job at South Bronx Legal Services. Her political activities continued to make her a lightning rod of controversy, and that may have contributed to her losing her position. As with many families, the loss of a job cascaded into the loss of a normal and pro-tected world. Mutulu had left home in Harlem because he was being pursued by the FBI for armed robbery and conspiracy. So, the Shakurs lost their apartment, and soon after, Afeni, Tupac, and Sekyiwa were headed to Baltimore, Maryland, in search of a new life. Aunt Glo watched them leave on a bus from New York's Port Authority. Tupac waved good-bye to her from the bus window, and she could see that his face was filled with confusion and hurt.

The family moved into a small and deteriorating house on Greenmount Avenue in East Baltimore with little heat and plenty of rats. This was the first time the family found itself in a slum. Afeni went on welfare, and she began to struggle to feed her children. The family now shopped for furniture and clothes at the Salvation Army and Goodwill. Almost all the Black Panthers were imprisoned or hiding, and there was no one to help her out. There was no other Afeni to lead a rally against this injustice and poverty. She often could not pay their bills, and the lights and phone were cut off. Tupac was teased at the Rolling Park Junior High School about his clothes, and he was called a bum. He later said in *Tupac: Resurrection,*

> Poverty. If I hated anything, it'd be that. The same crime element that white people are scared of, black people are scared of. . . . So we defend ourselves from the same crime element that they scared of, you know what I'm saying? So while they waiting for legislation to pass, and everything, we next door to the killer . . . What is that? We need protection too.

Tupac had not been raised to be easily defeated. When the lights were cut off, he went outside and read books and wrote in his journal by the dim glow of the streetlights. He found riches at the Salvation Army—an art book on Vincent van Gogh, a small record player, and an album by Don McLean. He wrote poetry about van Gogh and he played the record until the grooves wore through. With Afeni's help, he began to see that self-worth was far more valuable than external worth. So, he took his old jeans and denim jacket and added graffiti art to them. He started a trend. He took what life gave him and transformed it.

THE FIRST HIP-HOP

The origins of hip-hop are as varied as the music itself. One widely accepted origin story says that Jamaican clubs and

This still from the documentary *Tupac: Resurrection* shows Tupac Shakur as a young boy. After an intellectually and culturally stimulating childhood in New York City, Tupac was moved to Baltimore. The move had a profound impact on him.

dance halls had masters of ceremonies ("MCs" or "emcees") to introduce bands or "toast" disc jockeys they worked with. The MC usually used rhyming lyrics to warm up the crowd, punching out the words to a drum-and-bass beat that varied according to the music being introduced or the mood of the crowd. The MC usually spoke between songs, telling the audience to dance or shouting out greetings. When more and more Jamaicans moved to New York in the 1970s, more of their music and beat-rhymes moved with them. At block parties and park gatherings, a DJ or MC grabbed the microphone and work the crowd.

Tupac had heard the sounds since he was very young in New York, and he had always loved to rhyme with a beat with his cousins and friends during his childhood performances and later at parties. Now these same rhythmic styles were moving up and down Route 95 from Boston to Washington, D.C., and being combined with a variety of rhythm and blues, or R&B, songs.

Tupac found he could do less fighting with his fists and more with his words when he grabbed the mic at parties and dances and rapped out his rhymes on sex and violence. He began to be known as MC New York in his tough neighborhood, and he was getting respect for his poetry and rapping style. When a friend was killed on the streets, he organized a Stop the Violence march that grew to hundreds of people. He began to organize parties where music and the hip-hop beat-rhymes both entertained and raised awareness of black identity. The Black Panther movement lived in him, but it was translated into the new language of rap. Like all artists, he started reshaping what had been given to him and making it new.

THE BALTIMORE SCHOOL FOR THE ARTS

One day, a stray dog was hit by a car in front of where the Shakurs were living in Baltimore. Tupac carried the dog inside his house and treated its wounds. Eventually, he nursed the dog back to health. A retired couple living a few blocks away were impressed by Tupac's compassion. They began to talk to him, and he found that one of them had been a teacher at the Baltimore School for the Arts. Afeni urged him to apply there, and Tupac went for an audition. He was immediately accepted as a sophomore, and it changed his life. Biographer Jamal Joseph told this part of Tupac's story:

> The program opened a world of creative possibilities, and Tupac immersed himself fully. "Those white kids had things we had never seen," Tupac remembered. "That was the first time I saw that there were white people who you could get along with. Before that, I just believed what everyone else

said, that they were devils. But I loved it. I loved going to school. It taught me a lot. I was really starting to feel like I really wanted to be an artist."

One of the best things about going to the school was the other students. A beautiful young girl named Jada Pinkett (later to become Jada Pinkett Smith) became his lifelong friend after they appeared in several school productions together. They both threw themselves into whatever performance they were doing. They inspired each other—no half-hearted efforts for them. He later wrote a poem that called her "the foundation 4 my conception of love." She later said they had a "once-in-a-lifetime" friendship.

The pain of being uprooted from New York and being thrown into a rat-infested slum began to be replaced by a sense of accomplishment, of possibilities for happiness and security through art. In *Tupac: Resurrection* he recalled that at the school "We were exposed to everything. Theater, ballet, different people's lifestyles, royalty from other countries and things, everything."

Tupac became a minor celebrity at the Baltimore School for the Arts. He was writing and performing rap songs, a new genre of art that brought attention to the school. He won rap competitions, and as one of its brightest new talents, he was even used as a fund-raiser by the school. However, there was a problem. Tupac had not taken enough math courses to graduate. No one had kept track of his academic requirements. Afeni was furious. While they debated what to do, a piece of Afeni's New York life dropped on them.

ANOTHER CULTURE: CALIFORNIA IN 1988

Geronimo Pratt, Tupac's Black Panther godfather, was heading into a crucial phase in his trial and appeals process on the West Coast for conspiracy and murder. Afeni knew his case

Tupac met Jada Pinkett, shown here in 1996, at the Baltimore School for the Arts. The two began a friendship that lasted until Tupac's death. Pinkett went on to become a respected actress and, with husband Will Smith, one of Hollywood's power couples.

as well as anyone. She realized she needed to help. He had a new attorney, a young lawyer named Johnnie Cochran, who was very aggressive in mounting Pratt's defense, using every resource he could. Cochran used a defense he later became famous for in the case of O. J. Simpson—he said his client may have been framed by law enforcement officers. Pratt had been the head of the Los Angeles chapter of the Black Panthers, and his case had been moved to California. Afeni wanted to follow the case and decided to move to California. She had not found satisfying work in Baltimore, and her family was living in a slum. They all needed a change. Since Tupac was not going to get his diploma from the Baltimore School of Arts, she felt her children had nothing to lose and something to gain. California was still beckoning many in America—people looking for better jobs, warm sunshine almost year-round, and a laid-back culture.

In 1988, when Tupac was 17, Afeni and her family moved to Marin City, California. Marin City was a complicated place. Located just north of San Francisco, it was surrounded by some of the most beautiful homes and scenery in the country. However, Marin City itself had a depressed urban area; some have called where Tupac and his family moved "the Jungle," a set of Marin City low-rent housing projects and other places that attracted even more drug dealers and street gangs than the Baltimore slum the Shakurs had left.

Despite his surroundings, Tupac did what he usually did— he made the best of what he had. He enrolled as a junior in Tamalpais High School, known at Tam High. The school drew students from both Mill Valley, a mostly white and affluent section of Marin County, and Marin City. It was an example of what was best about school integration, bringing different kinds of students together. White kids, black kids, rich kids, and poor kids lived and learned together. Still, it was a typical high school, and he would have changed it in many ways, as he explained in *Tupac: Resurrection:*

I chase girls and want the car and loud music. But I like to think of myself as socially aware. I think there should be a drug class, a sex education class. A real sex education class. A class on police brutality. There should be a class on apartheid. There should be a class on why people are hungry, but there are not. There are classes on . . . gym. Physical education. Let's learn volleyball.

Tupac was not afraid of change, or of people of a different background and color, so he made friends with some of the Mill Valley kids. One of those kids was named Liza, and he did an answering-machine message for her in hip-hop style. Her older sister, Molly, became a friend as well and later became his personal assistant. Molly used Tupac as part of her English class project, interviewing him as though she were a real journalist and he a world-famous actor and rapper. In the mock interview, Tupac said many things that later came true. He knew he was going to change the world, and everyone he knew well bought into that knowledge and self-assurance. He inspired people with his directness and unbridled optimism.

Tupac improved Tam High's drama department by performing in several productions (although he didn't like to rehearse and frustrated some drama teachers in the process). He brought his intensity about black culture to the school, helping educate even the teachers about Malcolm X, Mutulu Shakur, and Geronimo Pratt. He got more serious about his rapping. He wrote an interesting paper in English Composition II called "Conquering All Obstacles," in which he said "our raps not the sorry-story raps everyone is so tired of. They are about what happens in the real world. Our goal is [to] have people relate to our raps, making it easier to see what really is happening out there. Even more important, what we may do to better our world."

LIVING IN THE JUNGLE

The Jungle had ways of wearing a family down, and illegal drugs and their dealers were an enemy that became powerful and relentless. Afeni never did drugs in New York or Maryland, but after moving to the Jungle she became addicted to crack. The 1980s had seen the drug take over many of America's urban areas, and the war on drugs seemed to be fought without many victories in places like Marin City. Tupac confronted his mother, and she told him the truth. He was angry and heartbroken. The greatest source of strength in his life had itself become weakened.

Tupac dropped out of Tam High at around the same time he learned about his mother's drug addiction. He soon moved out of her house, and Sekyiwa returned to New York to live with Aunt Glo. Now, at age 17, he was on the street or staying with friends, making do with what he could. He slept on couches and floors. He became depressed and disillusioned for the first time in his life. He felt broken. In *Tupac: Resurrection* he remembered this time:

> I was broke, nowhere to stay. I smoked weed. I hung out with the drug dealers, pimps and the criminals. They were the only people that cared about me at that point. And I needed a father—a male influence in my life, and these were males. My mom, she was lost at that particular moment. She wasn't caring about herself. She was addicted to crack . . . I didn't have enough credits to graduate. I dropped out . . . Then the dope dealers used to look out for me. They would just give me money and be like "Don't get involved in this. Get out there and do your dream."

Tupac always knew the healing power of his art. He could turn his pain into song. He could turn the reality of crack babies and lost souls into a kind of music people believed. He filled his notebooks with poems, songs, rhymes, and insights.

In 1997, after 27 years in prison, Elmer "Geronimo" Pratt was freed as a result of an overturn of his 1972 murder conviction. It was determined that Pratt was not given a fair trial and that an FBI informant who testified against him had lied under oath. Reflecting the turbulent time in U.S. history, Pratt was considered by some to be a political prisoner.

He became a well-known MC at block parties and gatherings. He perfected a hip-hop flow, a torrent of words with unmistakable anger, love, revolutionary spirit, and idealism all mixed together. The drug dealers and street people around him got to know about his gifts, and they protected him. They seemed to know he was going to escape their life, and a piece of them would live in him wherever he went. Biographer Jamal Joseph described Tupac in 1989:

> "Drug dealers were my sponsors," said Tupac. They never asked for anything in return. One actually paid for a couple of songs on Tupac's demo ... Dealers and people on the street always saw something special in Tupac. He read books and broke down politics in terms they could understand ... They recognized that Tupac would do great things, and their way of participating in that greatness was to keep Pac from getting too deep in the street game.

Tupac's style of rapping became even more direct during this time. He didn't want to rhyme about a world he didn't know. He knew enough about secure and protected people and their lives to know he was traveling on a different road. He knew that his art was all that stood between him and chaos, but that life had been difficult for many artists and revolutionaries. His poem "Nightmares" reflects this:

> I pour my heart in2 this poem
> and look 4 the meaning of Life
> the rich and powerful always prevail
> and the less fortunate strive though life
> MISTAKES R MADE 2 BE 4given
> we R 2 young 2 stress and suffer
> The path of purity and positivity
> has always ridden rougher

THE BLACK PANTHER PARTY

The 1960s are well known as one of America's most turbulent times. One source of that turbulence was an organization called the Black Panther Party for Self-Defense, later just called the Black Panther Party. It continues to be one of the most controversial facets of America's twentieth century.

The party was formed in Oakland, California, in 1966 (a year after Malcolm X had been killed and partly in reaction to his death) by two men, Huey Newton and Bobby Seale. They had two fundamental beliefs at first: applying the political theory of Karl Marx's call for social revolution by those at the bottom of the economic scale against those at the top and the saying of Chinese Communist leader Mao Tse-tung that "political power flows from the barrel of a gun." They wanted to assert (violently, if needed) the right of African Americans to defend themselves and to right the wrongs of poverty, hunger, and malnutrition-related diseases in black communities. The organization quickly gained strength and followers, mostly African Americans but soon also some other people locked out of the American dream of material wealth and security.

By 1967, only a year later, Federal Bureau of Investigation director J. Edgar Hoover declared that the Black Panthers were the most dangerous known threat to the country and led a war on them by creating a program called COINTELPRO designed to discredit, fight, and disarm the Panthers. Many Panthers were arrested on many different charges, usually including conspiracy, and many became locked into a justice system that caged them in prison. The most notorious cases were the "Chicago Eight," accused of conspiracy to disrupt the 1968 Democratic Convention, and the "New York 21," accused of conspiracy to bomb public places. All were eventually acquitted.

The most famous show of support for the party was when American Olympic medalists Tommie Smith and John Carlos raised their black-gloved fists in a Black Panther Party salute at the 1968 Olympics medals ceremony. A crucial battle in the war between law enforcement (FBI and local police) and the Black Panther Party occurred on December 4, 1969, when Panther leader Fred Hampton and another Panther were killed in their beds during a police raid on Hampton's Chicago home. Some historians believe that more than 40 Black Panthers were killed between 1968 and 1971, along with an almost equal number of police officers and police informants.

The death blow to the Black Panthers was probably dealt from within. The party split into two factions, the Black Power faction led by Stokely Carmichael and Eldridge Cleaver, and the Power to the People faction led by Newton and Seale. The Black Power faction urged more effective guerilla fighting against law enforcement, and the Power to the People faction wanted more focus on free medical clinics and community programs for drug rehab and sickle-cell anemia testing. It was an East Coast–West Coast rivalry (Newton in the West, Carmichael in the East) that would later play itself out again among rappers.

Enough Black Panthers survived to have a 40-year reunion in Oakland in 2006. The party still exists in various other forms and by other names, even in other countries, but few expect a return to the force that struck fear in the hearts of America's political and law enforcement leaders.

Afeni and Tupac hit rock bottom together, even though they were apart. She was broke and sick. He was broke and desperate. She later wrote in her autobiography that, "I was dying and I knew that I was dying because my spirit was not there at all. I would go to bed at night and not really care whether I woke up." She knew she could no longer protect her children, and it almost killed her. Tupac knew he had lost his mother, and it almost destroyed him. They both climbed out of this pit, and would soon climb mountains.

Fame and Infamy

One day, Tupac was walking on a street in Marin City and saw that a flower had pushed its way through the concrete sidewalk. He began to think about the power that this seemingly frail object must have, its will to live and find light. He called it his "ghetto rose" and he would later name a book of his poetry after it: *The Rose that Grew from Concrete*. His own will to live needed to be as strong as the rose, he knew. He now found a light in his life, and he cracked the concrete.

LEILA AND THE DIGITAL UNDERGROUND

Leila Steinberg was a poet and teacher living in Marin County, and one day, Tupac met her in a park and they began to talk. She read some of his poems, and she encouraged him at exactly the moment he needed encouragement. Steinberg asked him to come and live at her home, and she has kept copies of the books he read there—J. D. Salinger's *Catcher in the Rye*, Jamaica Kincaid's *At the Bottom of the River*, and Eileen Southern's *Music of Black Americans*, among many others. She soon offered to become an agent for him and his work, and she arranged for him to perform some of his songs at the 1989 Marin City Festival. Many of the San Francisco area's best artists and musicians were there, and the audience was huge. The crowd loved Tupac's work and that of the group he had formed with Ray Luv and DJ Dize called Strictly Dope. The event was a breakthrough for him. He was now rapping everywhere he could. He would interrupt conversations and just start rapping.

Steinberg later told reporter Malcolm Gladwell how impressive Tupac was at this time. In an article for the *Washington Post* in 1993, she said, "He is one of the most fragile people I ever met. He was so self-educated. He was the most articulate 17-year-old I had ever known. He had such an understanding of history and our system."

Steinberg introduced him to Atron Gregory, the manager of a Bay Area rap band named Digital Underground, who then introduced Tupac to the band's leader, Shock G. Tupac offered to do whatever was needed to help the band and soon was hired as a roadie (helper) and backup dancer. Shock G saw how Tupac connected with crowds when he warmed up the audience with his lyrics and dancing. Before long, Tupac was a full-fledged member of the band. In 1990, he went on tour with them, and when he was done he was wealthy enough to buy a Toyota Celica. He later told his biographer Jamal Joseph, "Shock G's responsible for all my success."

Tupac recorded one of his songs, named "Same Song," in a studio recording session as a member of the Digital Underground. The song was released as part of the album *This Is an EP Release* in 1991, and the song and album were hits. Tupac then appeared in his first video sitting on a throne and dressed in an African king's robes. The costume seemed to fit well. He was part of one of the hottest rap groups in the world, and he had helped make it even hotter. He also knew, however, that DU's fun-loving songs were good for parties but didn't express his outrage at social injustices. He knew his community was filled with violence, drugs, and despair. He was sure he had to record on his own to show what was happening in his America. Tupac spoke for young black men when few others would.

THE APOCALYPSE

Interscope Records was a company owned by a former John Lennon producer named Jimmy Iovine, along with a very wealthy man named Ted Field, an heir to the enormous Marshall Field (a chain of department stores) fortune. Interscope was looking for new rap artists since the music was becoming so popular that no record company could meet the demand with their existing artists. Rap supply was low, and rap demand was high. Interscope signed Tupac.

MC Hammer, Vanilla Ice, and New Kids on the Block now had to make way for a new sound. Snoop Dogg, Ice-T, and N.W.A. began to blast away at feel-good music and images. Tupac led some of the blasting—his debut album appeared in November 1991, and it was like a fire alarm in the night. He rapped about black revolutionaries in "Trapped," the need to fight violence with violence (one of the early messages of Malcolm X), and teen pregnancy in "Brenda's Got a Baby." The album was named *2Pacalypse Now,* and it never let up on the abuses and no-win situations many young people of color faced. True to both his warrior poet nature and his Black Panther legacy, the album was filled with the need to fight back against oppression. Like Joseph Conrad's *Heart of Darkness* and the movie based on the book, Francis Ford Coppola's *Apocalypse Now,* the horror of one group of people systematically exploiting and even killing another group was explored graphically and painfully.

Executives at Interscope Records, cofounded by Jimmy Iovine *(above)* recognized Tupac's talent and signed him to the label. Iovine had been a successful pop music producer, having worked with John Lennon, Bruce Springsteen, and U2, before heading up a record label. Tupac was later signed to Death Row Records, a subsidiary of Interscope.

2Pacalypse was released on October 12, 1991, and the sound rang loud and clear. It also alarmed many. In April 1992, the lawyer for a car thief named Ronald Ray Harper claimed that his client had killed a Texas state trooper because the album was playing in his car and incited him to commit murder. Republican vice president Dan Quayle gave a speech denouncing Tupac's kind of rap music, now labeled as "gangsta." Some people feel threatened by almost anything unfamiliar, and fear does not usually lead to clear thinking. Some voices in government and law enforcement said the new rap had no place in society. They were the voices of fear.

Jamal Joseph captured Tupac's response in his biography:

> Tupac was fearless and unapologetic. "And the raps that I'm rapping to my community shouldn't be filled with rage? . . . The media they don't talk about it, and it seems foreign because there's no one else talking about it." Law enforcement officials across the country also joined in on the attacks against Tupac and lyrics they said endorsed cop killing. This marked the beginning of Tupac's becoming a target of government and law enforcement. It was also a tremendous street endorsement for a "young nigga who was keeping it real." On street corners and blacktop basketball courts across the country, folks in the 'hood were relating to Tupac as a young ghetto troubadour who was making rhymes and music about their lives and their struggles.

THE PRICE AND VALUE OF FAME

Tupac was now becoming famous—and infamous. Soon after *2Pacalypse Now* was released, he was stopped in October 1991 by Oakland police for jaywalking. Words were exchanged, since Tupac felt he was being harassed. His jaywalking ticket quickly escalated to an arrest and physical restraint. Tupac came out of the confrontation with a cut on his right cheek that became a scar he would have for the rest of his life. Tupac filed a $10 million lawsuit against the city and knew he had a case. He had been around enough trials to know what his rights were. Eventually, all charges against him were dropped and he was paid $42,000 by the city.

Trouble now stalked Tupac like an evil shadow. He had become famous and attracted more "friends" who spent time with him. Some were old friends, but some were new and just wanted to hang around him. Some of these people would now get him in more trouble. In August 1992, two groups opened fire on each other after an outdoor Tupac concert in Marin City. People in both groups knew him, and when a six-year-old boy named Qa'id Walker-Teal was hit by a stray bullet and died, Tupac was devastated but blamed by some. He was never linked to the shooting, but trouble has a way of sticking to the most famous member of a group when things go bad.

Fame also tends to multiply itself. Tupac was always interested in acting and landed a small role in a movie called *Nothing but Trouble.* Soon he was on to bigger parts when he got a crucial role in the movie *Juice,* a story about four teenage friends in Harlem trying to stay out of trouble but not succeeding. Tupac played a character named Bishop, whose self-destructive actions become a center of the movie. In *Tupac: Resurrection,* he talked about the part and about moviemaking:

> Bishop is a psychopath, but, more true to this character, Bishop is a lonely, misguided young kid. His heroes are James Cagney and Scarface, those kinds of guys. Shoot-'em-up, go-out-in-a-blaze type of gangsters. I don't think acting is as technical as they try to make it . . . All you have to do is feel for your character and relate to your character. Because when you act you satisfy something inside of yourself.

To critics, Tupac was so good at playing Bishop that many wrote that a part of him must have known exactly what drives

The movie *Juice* gave Tupac an opportunity to create a full character on film. His talents surprised and impressed critics, and the public sat up and took notice of Tupac as an actor. In this still from the 1992 film, Tupac faces off with costar Vincent Laresca.

Bishop. The movie was a success, and Tupac's fame multiplied. But there was always a price; for the rest of his life he felt he had to live up to the character, that he had to be Bishop—he always had to be ready to stand up and die.

Alternating art forms between recording music and acting in films seemed to suit Tupac. In 1992, he made his second album, *Strictly 4 My N.I.G.G.A.Z*, released in February 1993. He redefined "nigga" as "Never Ignorant Getting Goals Accomplished." The album fascinated fans because of its two kinds of songs. One was the party song "I Get Around," which included his bandmates from Digital Underground and rhymed about sexy women and rivers of champagne. The other was "Keep Ya Head Up," which encouraged young mothers to continue struggling to make good. Tupac had known both sides of life now and had experienced the contradictory roles of women. He was accused of hypocrisy in his views of women, but less biased people knew he was just recording contradictory truths as he knew them. Poets have often known that the opposite of true is not always false. It is often an opposed truth. The album went platinum.

POETIC JUSTICE

One of the hottest new directors in the early 1990s was John Singleton, whose film *Boyz N the Hood* had taken American by storm. Singleton admired Tupac's performance in *Juice* and

POETIC JUSTICE

A director's second movie is often his or her most difficult project. In the case of John Singleton, it was especially tough. His first movie, *Boyz N the Hood,* won him Oscar nominations as best director and best writer in 1991. He became celebrated as the new black voice in America, both street smart and extremely talented. Everyone wanted to work with him. He wanted to work with Tupac Shakur, to provide the rapper with his first starring movie role.

John Singleton didn't want to follow *Boyz N the Hood* with a simple sequel—he had bigger ambitions. Instead, he made a film that celebrated the creative effort as a means of saving both individuals and their communities. The film was called *Poetic Justice.*

signed him to play a character named Lucky, a struggling but heroic single father, in his new movie, *Poetic Justice*. Singleton told reporters, "Cross-culturally, he's this generation's James Dean. He's a cautionary romantic figure for young people to watch and learn from." One of the most famous pop music stars, Janet Jackson, signed on to play the leading role, a character named Justice whose complicated life was enriched by poetry and art.

Hollywood buzzed about the pairing—two of the brightest talents in music crossing over into film and creating a strong relationship onscreen. Singleton was gambling by not using veteran actors for the roles. The gamble paid off. Almost everyone who saw *Poetic Justice* saw two sympathetic figures exploring their love for each other. The reviews were positive, and the box office receipts proved there was an audience for a romantic film with two black actors who did not have extensive

Janet Jackson played the role of Justice, a beautician whose lover has been killed by a gang in South Central Los Angeles and whose mother has committed suicide. The words of her own poetry are all she has to cling to. She meets a postal worker named Lucky, played by Tupac, whose world is also hanging by a thread, but whose rap songs are an outlet for his anger and despair.

Justice and Lucky connect and recognize the poetic gifts each has. They break out of themselves and their limited lives and transform each other. The role of Lucky would be Tupac's one and only starring role; if he had lived, no doubt he would have had many more.

The film *Poetic Justice* broke many boundaries and was a box office success, thanks in large part to the talent and charisma of Tupac, who displayed a warmth and sensitivity he had not previously revealed to the public. Suddenly, Tupac showed his potential to be a leading man, and the motion picture industry had high hopes for his career.

acting experience. The term "poetic justice" usually means that in the end, virtue gets rewarded and vice punished, and the film lived up to its name. For Tupac, the warrior Bishop gave way to the poet Lucky. He said in *Tupac: Resurrection* that "Lucky is doing it the opposite way Bishop did. He's working, he's very responsible . . . He wants to set goals and accomplish them."

But the process of making the movie was not without problems. Jackson's agents had asked that Tupac take an HIV test before the shooting began, and Tupac was offended by the request. He refused, saying if their sex scenes were real, he would take four HIV tests. Tupac developed both a personal and working relationship with Jackson and hoped the friendship would continue beyond the shooting. As so often happens in Hollywood, the relationships that develop during the hard work and intimacy of performing together in a romance fall apart when the filming stops. Often, somebody gets hurt. In this case, it was Tupac. But, as always, he moved on, knowing more and learning from his experiences. He always tried to come back stronger.

TRIPLE TROUBLE

The year 1993 was a defining but destructive one for Tupac. He was 22 years old. The wheel of fortune that had given him hit albums and hit movie roles at a young age now turned downward and gave him three misfortunes that would cost him for the rest of his life. The events defined the "thug life" part of his warrior code—fighting back when attacked, protecting yourself and your family and friends, no snitching, knowing who the real enemy is, making your word your bond. He now saw the word "outlaw" as standing for "Operating Under Thug Laws as Warriors." He was now becoming an outlaw.

In April 1993, Tupac got into a confrontation with another rapper during a concert in Lansing, Michigan. He swung a bat at the rapper and his friends to keep the fight from escalating further. He was arrested and given 10 days in jail.

On October 31, 1993, Tupac was driving in Atlanta, Georgia, with friends when he saw two white men heatedly arguing with a black motorist. The two white men were off-duty police officers (and brothers) named Mark and Scott Whitwell, and when Tupac stopped his car to see what

The year 1993 was a difficult one for Tupac, with a variety of charges brought against the successful rapper. An altercation with a rapper in Michigan led to 10 days in jail; an argument with two off-duty policemen led to the discharge of weapons; and the accusation of sexual assault led to a prison term. Above, Tupac is brought to a Manhattan police precinct after his arrest for the latter, on November 19, 1993.

was happening, they didn't identify themselves as officers. Soon, shots rang out. Only those involved know who started what—Tupac always maintained that he returned fire, not initiated it. Guns have a way of escalating such arguments quickly and often with deadly force. Investigators dropped charges against Tupac and his friends when it was found out that the off-duty officers probably were intoxicated and may have had a stolen gun. Tupac later said to *Vibe* magazine, "Where do I go to stay out of trouble? . . . There's not a place called Careful. I'm accessible, doing street rallies . . . That's why I'm getting into trouble."

The baseball bat and gun violence did not end up hurting Tupac nearly as much as what happened next. What sent him to jail for almost a year was sex. On November 14, 1993, Tupac and some friends went to a New York night club named Nell's. A 20-year-old woman recognized Tupac and came on to him in the middle of the dance floor. From there, their stories differ dramatically. Whether she stalked him and followed him days later to his hotel room where some of his friends had sex with her while he slept, or whether she was invited to the room and then raped by Tupac and his friends, only those present know for sure. What matters legally is that he was arrested and indicted on several charges, including sexual assault and unlawful weapons possession. He was set free on $50,000 bail.

Biographer Jamal Joseph wrote about Tupac's reactions to the incident:

> "I felt like I put my life on the line. At the time I made 'Keep Ya Head Up,' nobody had no songs about black women. I put out 'Keep Ya Head Up' from the bottom of my heart. It was real and they didn't defend it. I felt like it should have been women all over the country talking about 'Tupac couldn't have did that.' And people was actually asking me 'Did you do it?'"

Trouble had found him, and he had found trouble. His warrior nature and his warrior code had collided with a society that only wanted warriors for other battles. He was famous and infamous at the same time. As a reaction to his horrible year of 1993, he formed the group Thug Life with his stepbrother, Mopreme, and friends named Big Syke, Macadoshis, and Rated R. His warrior nature was taking over, at least for now. The worst was yet to come. So was some of the best.

The Worst of Times, the Best of Times

Because of all his negative publicity, Tupac was dropped
from the film *Higher Learning,* directed by John Singleton.
Since he was out on bail for sexual abuse and weapons possession, he was considered too dangerous to have on set by the
insurance companies that protect the moviemaking process.
The role he landed instead was his most powerful. He played
Birdie in a movie named *Above the Rim,* a minor independent
classic directed by Jeff Pollack (and not subject to the same
insurance restrictions as *Higher Learning*). Birdie is a gang
leader and drug dealer who competes for control over a rising
new basketball star named Kyle. Birdie and Birdie's brother
Shep are in opposite camps, and the struggle for power over
the player is a gripping one. Tupac had to show a character

Tupac followed his successful turn in *Poetic Justice* as a gang leader in the independent movie *Above the Rim*. He also contributed to the soundtrack. This period proved to be creatively prolific for him.

who was both thug and damaged by his surroundings. He succeeded brilliantly.

The soundtrack for *Above the Rim* was more successful commercially than the movie itself and featured a hit by Tupac and his new group, Thug Life. The song "Pour Out a Little Liquor" helped the album to go double platinum. Tupac then collaborated with a number of young rappers on *Thug Life, Vol. 1*. He used his fame to help others get their own recognition. He was in the middle of a frenzy of work that made those around him astonished at his stamina. He even fit in a role in the movie *Bullet* with Mickey Rourke; they became friends on and off the set.

DEAR MAMA

Tupac's mother, Afeni, had struggled for years with her addictions. After successfully completing a 12-step program in a Norwalk, Connecticut, drug and alcohol treatment center, she reunited with her beloved son. Tupac was now dividing his time between homes in Atlanta, Georgia, and Los Angeles, California, and Afeni joined him in both places. She became a refuge for him, a person to come to in the middle of the storm of controversy, moviemaking, and recording. He was now inspired to write one of his most famous and touching songs, "Dear Mama." He described the highs and lows of her life and women of courage like her. The song became the hit of the album *Me Against the World*.

Afeni urged Tupac to reunite their family. Soon, Aunt Glo was helping with the cooking, and his cousins began to make more music with him. Katari, Mutah, Yaki, Fatal, and Malcolm became the rappers that would eventually form the group Outlawz.

GOOD WORKS

Reuniting with his mother healed a part of Tupac, and he began to travel from city to city attacking drive-by shootings, disrespect of women, drug dealing to children, and all black-on-black crime. He visited Mutulu Shakur and Geronimo Pratt, both in prison, to try to get their support for his messages. He called for black unity, in much the same way Malcolm X had done many years earlier. He was a new kind of Black Panther, more concerned with solving social problems with less violence and more media attention. Tupac was quoted in newspapers as saying, "We're going to start taking back our communities one by one."

Tupac met with leaders of both the Crips and the Bloods, infamous Los Angeles street gangs, to urge more diplomacy and responsibility. Part of his warrior code, the "Code of Thug Life," was to spare civilians and children. He urged that "senseless brutality" be stopped. He tried to have gangs define neutral territory. He was realistic and practical in what he asked of the gangs—not utopian reform but real changes that spared the lives of innocent people.

He met with gang leaders in Brooklyn to urge them to adopt more of the code. They needed to stop destroying the very neighborhoods in which they lived. They needed to respect those around them and treat them as they would be treated.

An 11-year-old fan of Tupac's named Joshua Torres was diagnosed with muscular dystrophy and was dying from an enlarged heart. When asked by his mother what she could do to make him feel better, he said that he wanted to speak to his hero, Tupac Shakur. Mrs. Torres did not have much hope that could happen, but she called WPGC radio and spoke with a promotions coordinator there. Within an hour, her son was on the phone with his hero. His father, Robert Torres, wrote about what happened in a published letter:

> During the conversation our son was having difficulties and Mr. Shakur told him to hang in there and "Keep Ya Head Up" which was Joshua's favorite song. . . . Mr. Shakur asked our son what else could he do for him and our son asked Mr. Shakur could he visit him. . . . At 8:00 PM Mr. Shakur arrived and spent over an hour beside our son holding him and comforting him as much as possible and expressing lots of sympathy for our son Joshua. . . . Later that evening forty five minutes after Mr. Shakur left our son Joshua passed away.

"I SAW WHITE, JUST WHITE"

In late November 1994, Tupac's trial for sexual assault, abuse, and weapons possessions was finally coming to a close. He had been out on bail for months, but he knew he could spend as much as 25 years in jail if convicted. On November 30, the lawyers for both sides had completed their arguments, and the judge let the jury go for the night. Tupac was working in a frenzy, as usual, and was headed for Quad Recording Studio in New York's Times Square to do a guest appearance on a record by rapper Little Shawn. When Tupac, his friend Stretch, his manager Freddie More, and another friend entered the lobby of the building, they didn't think too much about the two men wearing army fatigues hanging out there, neither of whom made eye contact with Tupac. The men suddenly pulled out 9mm handguns and ordered everyone to the floor. The friends with Tupac obeyed, but he didn't. He described the scene in his biography:

> I just could not get on the floor. They started grabbing at me to see if I was strapped. They said "Take off your jewels!" and I wouldn't take them off . . . They started kicking me, hitting me. I never said don't shoot. I was quiet as hell . . . then I felt something on the back of my head. I thought they'd stomped me or pistol-whipped me . . . I saw white, just white. I didn't hear nothin'.

He had been shot once while standing and four more times when he was on the floor. He had wounds in his thigh, groin, torso, arm, and scalp. Somehow, moving in shock and on adrenaline, he made it up to the recording studio and said "Yo, I just got shot. Call my mother and tell her." He was rushed into surgery at Bellevue Hospital and was very lucky not to have died. The doctor at Bellevue later explained that if the bullets had been of a slightly higher caliber, he would not have survived.

On November 30, 1994, on his way to a recording studio, Tupac was shot in the lobby by unknown men. Miraculously, Tupac survived the attack. Here, Tupac arrives at Manhattan Supreme Court on December 1, 1994, to face a sexual assault charge from the previous year.

His family rushed to his side. Afeni, Aunt Glo, Sekyiwa, and even his biological father, Billy Garland, came to his hospital bed. No one knew if he was going to live or die. Hundreds of fans and reporters swarmed outside the hospital. In an act of sheer will, he left the hospital and made it to his trial the next day, twelve hours after major surgery. But after his leg went numb, he was rushed to Harlem's Metropolitan Hospital. Later, the jury came back with a verdict of innocent on the weapons charge but guilty on the sexual assault charge. On February 7, 1995, he was sentenced to a prison term of one and a half to four and a half years in a maximum security prison in upstate New York, and he started serving his sentence on February 14.

A SOUL ON ICE

His lawyers were surprised and outraged that he was sent to the Clinton Correctional Facility in upstate New York, 320 miles north of Manhattan. Nicknamed "Little Siberia," it was a maximum-security prison for the worst of the worst. They felt he didn't belong anywhere near such a place.

Prison is an institution that some have called a crazy and violent combination of several other kinds of institutions. It is a bleak alcohol and drug abuse hospital, a harsh and all-too-real university, and a perverted monastery. But Malcolm X had used his prison time well, and Tupac was determined to do the same. "Malcolm X has said that the penitentiary has been a university to many a black man. If that's the case, I plan to come out with five PhDs," he told biographer Jamal Joseph. He would read and take to heart Niccolo Machiavelli's *The Prince*, whose message has been summarized as "it is better for a leader to be both loved and feared, but if he or she has to choose, it better to be feared." A classic of war strategy by the author Sun Tzu, *The Art of War*, was his constant companion. Clearly, he was preparing and feeding his warrior nature in prison. The poet side of his nature was in retreat.

Tupac was forced to give up drinking and smoking marijuana and using any other drugs. He tried to do 1,000 push-ups and 1,000 jumping jacks a day, and then added 500 sit-ups to his routine. He practiced his martial arts training and yoga as well. He meditated and read books at a dizzying rate. His frenzy of work did not stop just because he was in prison. He always worked hard.

Biographer Jamal Joseph wrote about this prison time:

> Tupac never asked for or received special treatment. In fact, the way the prison authorities treated him was more in line with his Black Panther legacy than his worldwide celebrity status. Rumors that Tupac was being pressured, harassed, or abused by other prisoners were unfounded. King Cuba Shaquawn, a street vendor and community activist who served time with Tupac, recalls that Tupac carried himself like a young Panther. "Tupac gave respect and got respect from everyone. He interacted with other prisoners and would get into heavy conversations about politics, music, life. Wherever you went, Tupac could go there with you."

Tupac gave out copies of Malcolm X's autobiography and told other inmates that Malcolm was a true hero. He spent time talking to other inmates about black history and what could be done to improve black communities when and if prisoners were released. He even confronted a member of the Aryan Brotherhood, a white supremacist group, and they actually explored each other's views without violence. "It blew my mind that we could be such totally different people, with such totally different world views and really talk and hear each other," Tupac told his biographer. Being in prison was a long exercise in anger management and a hard lesson in humility.

Being in prison can also be a desperately lonely time. A woman named Keisha Morris had met Tupac in a club a year before he went to prison, and they had become good friends.

The Notorious B.I.G. *(above)* **became Tupac's friend during the shooting of** *Poetic Justice,* **but the two rappers were rivals, thanks to the feuding record labels they were signed to. Tupac was convinced that Biggie and Sean Combs were behind his near-deadly shooting.**

She was an intelligent and gifted college student, and they talked about everything—politics, law, black history, cultural issues of all kinds. She was unlike many of the women he had known, and she visited him often in prison. In a sudden impulse to connect with a life outside prison and make a commitment to something, he married her on April 29, 1995. The strains of having a married life behind bars would eventually break their relationship, and they had their marriage annulled, but when they parted some six months later they remained friends.

The walls of the prison cells began to close in on Tupac, and he felt like a caged panther. He knew he needed to do anything to get out and begin the rest of his life. He tortured himself with the thought that he had been set up for his shooting by old friends. Up-and-coming rapper Christopher Wallace, known as the Notorious B.I.G. (and called "Biggie") and rap star Sean "Puffy" Combs had both been recording for Bad Boy Records at the Quad Studio the night Tupac was shot. Biggie and Tupac had become friends during the shooting of *Poetic Justice*, but they recorded for different companies and were also natural rivals. When Biggie released a song called "Who Shot Ya" about a shooting similar to Tupac's, Tupac's suspicions deepened that Biggie had something to do with the attacks on him. At first, an East Coast–West Coast rivalry between Bad Boy Records (on the East Coast, started by Sean Combs when he was still in college) and its artists (Biggie, Puffy, and many others), and a company called Death Row Records (producing artists like Tupac, Snoop Dogg, and many others on the West Coast) had seemed like innocent sport. It was now turning deadly serious.

ON TO DEATH ROW

A man named Marion Knight also became a regular prison visitor. Knight, called "Suge" (short for his childhood nickname "Sugar Bear"), was an enormous man who owned Death Row Records. He was a powerful figure in the rap recording industry and had produced works by legends Dr. Dre and Snoop Dogg. He had done time in prison and knew what it could do to an inmate's mind and body.

He made Tupac an offer he couldn't refuse. Knight would pay the $1.4 million appeal bond that would release Tupac from jail, if Tupac would record three albums for Death Row Records. In the prison waiting room a contract was drawn up on a paper napkin between the two. Tupac signed it on September 16,

Death Row Records chairman Suge Knight (*above,* with Tupac on August 15, 1996) bailed Tupac out of jail in exchange for the rapper's next three records. Knight and Tupac actively encouraged the East Coast–West Coast rivalry in the rap world, which resulted in the death of Tupac, a nine-year prison sentence for Knight, and the end of Death Row Records.

1995, and was released from prison on October 10, 1995. He had served about eight months of his term.

When he walked out of the Clinton Correctional Facility, Tupac took a long deep breath and held it for what seemed like an eternity. Then he looked back at the prison and gave it the middle finger. He boarded a flight for Los Angeles, where he checked into the Peninsula Hotel in Beverly Hills. He would never take luxury for granted again.

He showered and changed into clean clothes, then drove to a place he had dreamed of in prison, a restaurant named El Pollo Loco near Los Angeles. He traded prison food for champagne, filet mignon, lobster, and shrimp. He drove up and down the streets of L.A. He was free.

He asked that his mother and family come visit him, and then he went right to a recording studio and made the song "When I Get Free." He had no time to waste. He also needed money. He soon started a group called the Outlawz.

Tupac now worked with different producers with Death Row, including the famous Dr. Dre. They collaborated on "California Love," which had a sound that recalled the "wall of sound" beats of bands like Tower of Power and Earth, Wind & Fire. It was a love song, from Tupac to West Coast hip-hop. His friend Jada Pinkett came up with the idea to shoot a video for the song in a landscape that looked like one from a *Mad Max* movie, with warrior costumes and machine-gun-mounted cars. Death Row and MTV arranged a huge publicity event around the release of the song and video. Both were a hit. The song blared from radio stations and boom boxes around the country. Tupac was back. He had been out of prison less than three weeks and had written and produced 20 songs.

A FAMILY REUNITED

Tupac soon rented a house on the Pacific Ocean, in a place called the Malibu Colony. It was a magical location, home to many stars. Soon his nieces Ismani and Nzingha and his nephews Malik and Carl were either living there or visiting often. When Tupac called out, "Ma, can I have a soda?" Afeni was usually nearby to bring him his favorite, Sunkist Orange. He was now close with his mother and aunt again, and he never appreciated them more. He didn't have many friends, he later said, only family. Many of the friends he thought he

MALIBU COLONY

When Tupac moved to the Malibu Colony, he experienced some of the happiest times of his life. Malibu Colony is a famous address. It started as a private beach residence owned by a family of millionaires grown rich from their stock in the Union Oil Company. Armed guards rode horses up and down the beach to keep out trespassers wanting to get on some of the most beautiful beaches in the world. When the family needed money and began renting and then selling pieces of the 27-mile beachfront properties on the Pacific Coast north of Los Angeles, the rich and famous flocked to the Colony. Tom Hanks, Sting, Bill Murray, and many others have owned homes there. Star Leonard DiCaprio would rather rent—about $50,000 per month for a nice house. Malibu itself is home to actors Danny DeVito, John Cusack, Courtney Cox, David Duchovny, Pierce Brosnan, Pamela Anderson, and Richard Gere. Musicians who live there include Barbra Streisand, members of Incubus, Josh Groban, Britney Spears, Diana Ross, and Axl Rose.

A popular Malibu license-plate holder reads, "Malibu: A Way of Life." Zip code 90265 is one of the most desirable addresses in the world. Residents and tourists debate about which is the best beach along the Malibu coast. Many have said that Zuma Beach is their favorite, and Malibu High School students like to play volleyball and party between lifeguard towers six and seven at Zuma.

had had abandoned him when he went to prison. Some of his friends, he thought, had tried to kill him. He trusted no one but family now.

His family extended to people he had known much of his life, the life he had before he became famous. His high-school friend Molly became his assistant. Former Black Panther and family friend Yaasmyn Fula became a close companion. Jamala, his cousin, liked to cook him his favorite dish—chicken wings. Afeni's curried shrimp was a close second. His family supported him, and he supported them. When other recording artists would send out for food during a long day at the studio, he got his food sent from home. He wouldn't have it any other way. He had gone through the worst of times and the best of times. Prison had taught him to cherish every second of time. It turned out, he wouldn't have much time left.

The Last Year: 1996

Tupac threw himself into work, as he usually did. No one would ever question his work ethic. He often was recording in one studio and listening to songs in another. He wanted to make new music, hot and cutting-edge sounds that struck him as true and real. His poet side wrestled to capture the feelings of love and freedom. His warrior side made him wary.

He wanted to get back into acting, but it seemed like no one would take a chance on this ex-con. Movie studios, or their insurance companies, were generally afraid of him. But one movie producer wasn't.

GRIDLOCK'D AND *GANG RELATED*

Hip-hop businessman Russell Simmons knew he had to take a chance on Tupac. Simmons owned Def Pictures, and he and

Released in 1997, the year after his death, *Gridlock'd* was a chance for Tupac to do a "buddy movie." He exhibited a winning chemistry with his costar, critically-acclaimed actor Tim Roth and, perhaps more surprisingly, a talent for comedic repartee. The *New York Times* review of the film praised Tupac's "appealing mix of presence, confidence and humor" and lamented that he "could have looked forward to a big future on the screen."

director Stan Lathan were impressed with Tupac's ideas about a character they were casting for a movie to be called *Gridlock'd*. A producer on the movie, Preston Holmes, was also smart enough to fight to get Tupac on board.

English actor Tim Roth (famous for playing one of the robbers in the restaurant scenes in the hit movie *Pulp Fiction*) would be one of the leads, and the character Spoon was the other. Both characters were drug addicts trying to get clean. Tupac got the part of Spoon and played it well. Everyone who worked with him later said he was a joy to work with—funny, intelligent, and always on time. Roth and Tupac joked that they were the new Mel Gibson and Danny Glover combination, except that Tupac was the Mel Gibson character and Roth the Danny Glover character from the *Lethal Weapon* movies.

Soon, Tupac shot what was to be his last movie, which would be released a year later. It was called *Gang Related* and starred James Belushi and Tupac as cops caught up in corruption and murder. It was called "gritty and effective" by several critics.

ALL EYEZ ON ME

During this period, Tupac took one of the biggest artistic gambles of his life. After he shot scenes from *Gridlock'd* he rushed to a recording studio to record or work on songs. He slept in whatever car was driving him between locations.

Snoop Dogg collaborated with him on "2 of Amerikaz Most Wanted," in which they expressed their feelings about being on trial for their lives. (Snoop had stood trial for murder, for which he was acquitted.) Songs were pouring forth thanks to all of Tupac's rage at being locked up, the hurt of betrayal, and his love for music.

Against the advice of Death Row Records and many other professionals, Tupac insisted on recording and releasing a double album, which he called *All Eyez on Me*. Double albums are a rarity and reserved for musical legends with an established buying audience. It was a bold move, and it worked. On February 16, 1996, a day after the album was released, Tupac got a call from Suge Knight telling him that the double album went platinum four hours after it was released. It was the first hip-hop double album, and it became one of the best-selling albums in hip-hop history—nine times platinum.

Many of its tracks are considered classics—"Ambitionz Az a Ridah," "I Ain't Mad at Cha," "California Love," "Life Goes on," and "Picture Me Rollin" mixed his warrior themes with his poet themes. The album was less confrontational than *Me Against the World*.

A DIVIDED NATURE

Tupac's warrior-poet nature now divided more than ever. The warrior became Makaveli, a character and stage name he created based on his readings of Niccolo Machiavelli's *The Prince*. Tupac played the part to challenge people and create controversy. It was a role that suited him at Death Row Records. He began making songs for an album to be called *The Don Killuminati: The 7 Day Theory*, which was so named because it had been written, recorded, and produced in one week. It was one of his darkest albums, focusing on pain and aggression.

He also began working on songs for a different kind of album, which he would label *Supreme Euthanasia*. If one set of songs could be angry and defiant, the other could be sad and even at peace. Tupac formed a company called Euphanasia, which was a combination of euphoria and euthanasia. For him, euthanasia meant not taking one's life but having the right to choose one's life. Euphanasia reportedly was intended as a movie production company. The company logo showed an angel armed to the teeth; its supply of ammunition resembled a keyboard. Songs were weapons. Poets were warriors.

Tupac's divided nature showed itself in many ways. When a friend of a friend was killed in a carjacking, the dead man's stepdaughter, Shana, was devastated. Tupac found out about

Rapper Snoop Dogg *(center)* **was a good friend of Tupac, and when the two became label mates they grew even closer, even collaborating on a recording. After the deaths of Tupac and the Notorious B.I.G., Snoop joined other rappers to promote peace within the hip-hop community.**

her loss and consoled her. When he later learned that she had no date for her high school prom, he took her. He made sure the limo and the flowers were just what she wanted. He prepared more for that prom night than he did for the Grammy Awards. Shana had the night of her young life.

He quietly raised money for a Los Angeles-based program, A Place Called Home, which provided counseling, tutoring, and health services to at-risk inner-city young men and women. Tupac did not just lend his name. He let every friend and acquaintance know that he expected their best efforts in helping the organization with time and money.

But he also could be capable of great hatred. In June 1996, he released the song "Hit 'Em Up," which was a full assault on Biggie, Bad Boy, and other East Coast rappers. He called them punks with no skills and claimed to the world that he had an affair with Biggie's wife, Faith Evans. A war had now started. Things were said and sung that could never be taken back in his lifetime.

GETTING OFF DEATH ROW

Suge Knight, the head of Death Row Records, made no secret about adding fuel to the growing fire between his artists and those of Bad Boy Records. The East Coast–West Coast rivalry was escalating, and it was good for business but bad for some people. Knight liked to show his West Coast affiliation with the L.A.-based gang the Bloods, wearing red and having his offices decorated in the gang's color. Tupac didn't like to take sides in this war. The more he pursued business ventures not related to Death Row, the more Knight tried to bring him back to recording only for his company. Tupac wanted to write an autobiography, tentatively called *Mama's Boy,* and even a cookbook. He hoped to work more on movies, eventually writing and directing them, not just acting in them.

Tensions between Knight and Tupac began to grow. Tupac could not understand why he was not collecting more money in royalties from his wildly successful albums. Death Row was run like many entertainment businesses, with many expenses charged against artists' royalties. As a result, the artists do not get the money they think they deserve. The film and recording industries are more creative with accounting than most.

Knight tried to calm his artist by sending him a Rolls-Royce and then a Hummer. It didn't work. When he couldn't get enough answers about his royalties, Tupac decided to leave

GOING GOLD, PLATINUM, AND DIAMOND

The Recording Industry Association of America (RIAA) is a powerful association. It keeps score in the music business. As long ago as 1942, RIAA awarded its first gold record to celebrate the selling of one million single records or an album that sold in excess of $1,000,000. The first winner was Glenn Miller, for a song named "Chattanooga Choo-Choo." In 1956, Elvis Presley received his first gold record, for "Hound Dog."

Soon, it became clear that an award for higher than a million in sales was needed. What was more valuable than gold? Platinum. The RIAA changed its standards, and in the 1960s, pronounced that gold was now awarded to either single records or albums (now CDs) that sold in excess of 500,000 units in the United States (including military bases abroad), and platinum for those that sold in excess of 1,000,000. In 1999, a third category was created: diamond, for units that sold over 10,000,000. By tradition, these unit sales are not actual sales figures. They record the numbers of records sent out to stores, not the number that people in the stores or online have actually bought.

Music videos have their own sales levels: 25,000 is gold for a single video; 50,000 for a long-form music video; 50,000 and 100,000 are platinum for single and long music videos; 100,000 and 200,000 are diamond.

What is the best-selling album of all time? It's by the Eagles, their *Greatest Hits* (1971–1975), which has sold 29X platinum (or 2.9X diamond). Second Place? Michael Jackson's *Thriller* at 27X platinum. *Led Zeppelin IV* is not far behind, and Pink Floyd's *The Wall* is currently in fourth place.

Death Row. On August 27, 1996, he faxed a letter to Knight saying that their business relationship was over.

FIGHT NIGHT: SEPTEMBER 7, 1996

There are few events in sports like heavyweight championship fights. On September 7, 1996, champion Mike Tyson fought challenger Bruce Seldon at the MGM Grand Hotel in Las Vegas, Nevada. Reverend Jesse Jackson had good seats to the fight, as did rappers MC Hammer and members of Run-DMC. Knight wanted to make peace with his star rapper and had invited Tupac to come to Vegas as his ringside guest, in hard-to-get $1,000 seats. Tupac reluctantly agreed. He wanted to break from Death Row Records and Knight, but he also loved boxing and couldn't stay away from a Tyson fight. He had written songs for Tyson, and one was playing over the hotel loudspeakers as Tyson entered the ring: "Wrote the Glory."

Tupac sat in section 4, seat 2, row E, near actors Charlie Sheen and Louis Gossett Jr., and along with the 16,000 other spectators watched as Tyson destroyed Seldon in less than two minutes. The fight was over before some had taken their seats.

Knight, Tupac, bodyguard Frank Alexander, and some other friends then walked through the casino lobby of the MGM Grand, and once again trouble found Tupac. A man named Orlando "Baby Lane" Anderson was in their path, and someone recognized him as a member of the Los Angeles gang the Crips, who had grabbed a Death Row Records medallion off of an acquaintance of Knight's and Tupac's a few months earlier. (The Crips are rivals to the Bloods.) Reports are contradictory on exactly what happened next, but many agree that Tupac grabbed a medallion on Anderson's neck and in the process knocked Anderson down. Some of the Death Row group then kicked Anderson, stopping only when MGM security guards rushed in. Surveillance cameras then show that Tupac and his group walked away without being questioned. Anderson declined to file a complaint.

The night of Tupac's murder, he attended the WBA heavyweight championship fight between Mike Tyson *(left)* **and Bruce Seldon.**

Tupac then walked back to the Luxor Hotel, a block south of the MGM Grand, and changed his clothes from a silk shirt and tan slacks to a tank top and baggy jeans. His girlfriend, Kidada Jones (daughter of composer Quincy Jones), was in the hotel room with him, but she didn't come downstairs with him when he went out later with his bodyguard and others. Knight had called and convinced Tupac to come to his house in Paradise Valley, saying they would go together to Club 662, which was owned by Knight. Tupac, feeling that his life was in danger, sometimes wore a bulletproof vest or flak jacket, but the desert was too hot to consider it this time, and Tupac knew there was security at the club.

Suge Knight's black BMW, pocked by bullet holes, is shown above at the Las Vegas crime scene. Knight has been blamed for putting a hit on Tupac, but criminal charges have never been filed against him.

At about 10 P.M., an entourage of cars left Knight's house for Club 662, only a few miles away. Tupac rode in the passenger seat of Knight's 1996 750 BMW sedan, just purchased by Death Row. The car had chrome wheels, tinted windows, and a state-of-the art sound system that they cranked up. The caravan of cars—a Lexus, Miata, BMW wagon, and Mercedes, as well as Knight's car, carried friends and the bodyguard.

Tupac was looking forward to getting on stage with Run-DMC at Club 662. They were doing a benefit for a group dedicated to keeping children away from violence. The convoy headed east on Flamingo Road and came to a red light at Koval Lane, across from the Maxim Hotel. Four young women pulled up in a Chrysler sedan to the left of Knight's BMW and smiled at Knight and his passenger. To the right of the BMW, a Cadillac pulled up, and the rear driver-side window slowly rolled down. A burst of bullets from a semiautomatic handgun hit the BMW. Thirteen bullets were later recovered by police. Three of them lodged in Tupac—one in his chest, one in his hip, and one in his right hand. Journalist Cathy Scott did extensive research on the shooting for her book, *The Killing of Tupac Shakur,* and she tells the story from there:

> The gunfire ended as quickly as it had begun. The shooting of Tupac Shakur, executed in cold blood, was over in a matter of seconds.
>
> "You hit?" Suge asked Tupac.
>
> "I'm hit," Tupac answered . . .
>
> Suge had a flip Motorola cellular telephone with him, but he didn't use it to call 911 for help. With adrenaline pumping and Tupac bleeding heavily as he sat slumped in the front seat, Suge somehow managed to make a U-turn in heavy traffic, even though his car now had two flat tires . . .
>
> Suge and Tupac made it onto the Strip. Sirens from patrol cruisers, ambulances, a fire rescue unit, and the highway patrol screamed as every unit converged on the scene . . . When the paramedics arrived, the mortally wounded Tupac was being lifted out of the front seat by Suge Knight and Frank Alexander. They placed him on the ground.
>
> Tupac was conscious, but short of breath . . . "I can't breathe," Tupac kept repeating . . . Suge climbed in [to the ambulance] and sat on a bench next to the gurney. Just as paramedics were closing the back doors to the ambulance, witnesses heard Tupac quietly say, "I'm dyin', man."
>
> His words were prophetic: Tupac Amaru Shakur would succumb to his wounds six days later.

The Legacy
of a Warrior
Poet

On Friday, September 13, 1996, at 4:03 P.M., Tupac Shakur's life ended at the University Medical Center of Southern Nevada. His official cause of death was cardiac arrest and respiratory failure after he was taken off a life-support system. The Las Vegas Metropolitan Police Department never officially solved the case, but off the record one policeman told journalist Cathy Scott he thought Tupac had been killed by Southside Crips as revenge for the fight with Orlando Anderson. Many are not satisfied with that explanation, and some think that Biggie hired the Crips to carry out an execution as revenge for the East Coast–West Coast fighting. Some think Knight was the target that night, not Tupac. Stories swirled around that Knight had been targeted by the Crips and that

Although Tupac's murder shocked the world, in some ways it surprised no one. The senseless shooting seemed to epitomize the thug life glamorized in gangsta rap's lyrics. The urban art captured in the photograph above memorializes Tupac with the plea "Stop the Violence."

he owed Tupac $17 million in royalties, but nothing has ever been confirmed. A few conspiracy theorists believe Tupac is still living, but journalists who have seen and published the autopsy photos say that is impossible. Whoever is responsible, the killing of rappers still has not stopped, and Biggie himself was murdered soon after.

This still from *Gang Related* shows Tupac in a scene with James Belushi and Gary Cole. The film is notable for featuring Tupac's last appearance in a motion picture; it was released the year after his death.

REMEMBERING A LEGEND

No official public funeral for Tupac Shakur was ever arranged, but memorials were held in New York, Atlanta, and many other places. Thousands of people came to remember his music and poetry with dances, African drumming, gospel readings, and hip-hop songs. Afeni did not want people to mourn him, but to celebrate him. Thousands did and still do.

Tupac's music and influence live on stronger than ever. The *Guinness Book of World Records* lists Tupac as the best-selling hip-hop artist, having sold over 75 million albums worldwide. More songs have now been released after his death than while he was alive. He was inducted into the Hip-Hop Hall of Fame in 2002.

Shock G recalled that Tupac liked nothing better than spending a day at the studio experimenting, and even though Tupac may not have wanted all of these songs to be released, his fans are grateful. *The Don Killuminati: The 7 Day Theory* was released in November 1996. The movie *Gridlock'd* opened five months after Tupac died, to some of the best reviews he had ever received. Movie critics agreed that he would have had a brilliant career in films. On November 17, 1997, the album *R U Still Down?* was released, and it sold well. Since his death, eight CDs have appeared along with two albums by artists using his poetry. In 2003, a film about his life, *Tupac: Resurrection,* opened and was later nominated for an Academy Award. The movie's illustrated companion book by the same name tells his story in a fresh new way.

ALWAYS IN MIND

Tupac was the subject of a 2003 scholarly conference, sponsored by the Hip-Hop Archive at Harvard University, called "All Eyez on Me: Tupac Shakur and the Search for the Modern Folk Hero." Author Michael Eric Dyson, one of the scholars, wrote in *Black Issues Book Review* about the legacy of Tupac:

> One of the reasons Tupac still resonates in the culture is his outsized literary ambition. When it comes to the themes of his music, Tupac thought big, and often in stark binaries: life and death ("Life Goes On"); love and hate ("Hail Mary"); judgment and forgiveness ("I Ain't Mad at Cha"); joy and pain ("To Live and Die in L.A."); and heaven and hell ("I Wonder if Heaven Got a Ghetto"). He fearlessly, and poetically, explored dimensions of the male psyche rejected by his rap peers.

Dyson went on to note how many times Tupac wrote about a government that had plenty of money for wars but little to

Afeni Shakur-Davis *(above)* **attends a ceremony by the Tupac Amaru Shakur Foundation to honor her son on the tenth anniversary of his death. Shakur-Davis created the foundation in 1997 to bring arts training to young people. The foundation provides training in creative writing, acting, dance, spoken word, set design, and arts business management.**

feed poor people devastated by disasters. Economic inequality, racial profiling, teenage motherhood, absentee fathers, and the wrong political leadership were themes Tupac thought and wrote about that Americans still live with.

Scholars like Steven Pinker have noted that many people like Tupac live in a "culture of honor," where their society is beyond the reach of the law and precious assets are easily stolen. Men cultivate a hair trigger for violent retaliation to preserve the respect that is so important for protection. Scottish highlanders, Western cowboys, Sioux Indians, Balkan tribesman, and Masai warriors come from cultures of honor. So do many rappers.

THE LASTING FOUNDATION

Afeni has created the Tupac Amaru Shakur Foundation to carry on Tupac's legacy. It provides creative arts and leadership training to young people. The foundation's Creative Arts Center in Stone Mountain, Georgia, is a beautiful facility with a peace garden that has a fountain shaped like a cross. Tupac's biographer, Jamal Joseph, ends his book in a moving tribute, using Tupac's own words.

> Tupac once said, "I'm not saying I'm going to change the world. But I guarantee that I will spark the brain that will change the world." He lives on through his work, his art, his passion, and his uncompromising belief that freedom is living exactly the way you want to.

One of the most lasting gifts Tupac has given the world is the love he inspired. The greatest love of all was his for his mother, and hers for her son. Afeni has achieved a higher wisdom, and she explains some of it in the preface to Jamal Joseph's biography:

> Make ambitious goals, never give up, no matter what the circumstances. Choose to live! Choose to do for and save the children in your community. Always create, always think, always analyze . . . Give yourself permission to express your feelings in any way that suits you, be it through song, poetry, painting, acting, dance . . . When conflict arises, resolve it diplomatically . . . Remember, any coward can place a finger on the trigger of a gun and apply minimum pressure. However, it takes true character to methodically resolve your conflict non-violently.

Tupac Amaru Shakur's ashes were scattered behind his mother's home in Atlanta; in Aunt Glo's yard, on 125th Street between Seventh and Eighth Avenues in New York's Harlem, and on a beach in Malibu. These were the places he loved. More ashes may be scattered in South Africa later. But his legacy has been scattered all over the world. He lives on whenever a young child in Harlem gets a test for sickle-cell anemia, whenever a

TUPAC AMARU CENTER FOR THE ARTS

The Tupac Amaru Center for the Arts (known as TASCA) was founded by Afeni Shakur and opened in June 2005. It is located at 5616 Memorial Drive in Stone Mountain, Georgia, about 20 miles from Atlanta. This visitor center has many sights and sounds for Tupac fans, including art from people around the world who were inspired by him. A line of clothing called Makaveli, named after one of Tupac's sources of inspiration, Niccolo Machiavelli, is sold there, as are books, music, and other reminders of the great rapper.

The center has a peace garden, a peace trail, a bronze statue of Tupac, and outdoor pavilions for performances. Perhaps the most important part is the Performing Arts Program. It started as a summer camp in 1999, but is now year-round and gives students ages 12 to 18 a chance to develop their talents in singing, dancing, and acting. Creative writing, set and stage design, and other disciplines have recently been added. The program is very selective; auditions are rigorous.

Performers from the program have performed on *Good Day Atlanta,* the VH1's *Save the Music Battle of the Bands,* and the Source Awards. For more information, contact Celina Nixon or Carlos Coleman at (404) 298-4222.

His charisma and talent made him a star; his propensity for trouble made him a headline; and his early death made him a legend. A jumble of contradictions, Tupac was both heralded as a genius and derided as a gangsta thug. This complex character continues to captivate more than a decade after his life was cut short.

homeless person in Oakland receives a hot meal, and wherever his music is played. He was one of the warrior poets of our age and of ages to come.

Some of his most moving words show his followers that he knew something about what was going to happen to him. In the third verse of "Thugz Mansion," he becomes a prophet.

Dear mama don't cry
Your baby boy's doin' good
Tell the homies I'm in heaven and it ain't got hoods
Seen a show with Marvin Gaye last night
It had me shook
Drinking peppermint schnapps with Jackie Wilson
And Sam Cooke
Then some lady named Billie Holiday sang
Sittin' there kickin' it with Malcolm till the day came
Lil' Latasha sure grown
Tell the lady in the liquor store that she's forgiven
So come home
Maybe in time you'll understand
Only God can save us
Where Miles Davis cutting loose with the band
Just think of all the people that you knew in the past that
passed on
They in heaven found peace at last
Picture a place that they exist together
There has to be a place better than this
In Heaven
So right before I sleep dear God what I'm askin'
Remember this face save me a place
In Thugz Mansion

DISCOGRAPHY

STUDIO ALBUMS RELEASED WHILE ALIVE
2Pacalypse Now (1991) Gold
Strictly 4 My N.I.G.G.A.Z (1993) Platinum
Thug Life: Thug Life Volume 1 (1994) Gold
Me Against the World (1995) Double Platinum
All Eyez on Me (1996) 9X Platinum

STUDIO ALBUMS RELEASED POSTHUMOUSLY
The Don Killuminati: The 7 Day Theory (1996) 7X Platinum
R U Still Down? (Remember Me) (1997) 4X Platinum
Still I Rise (1999) Platinum
Until the End of Time (2001) 4X Platinum
Better Dayz (2002) 3X Platinum
Loyal to the Game (2004) Platinum
Pac's Life (2006) Gold

OTHER ALBUMS
Greatest Hits (1998) 9X Platinum
The Rose that Grew from Concrete (2000)
Nu-Mixx Klazzics (2003) Gold
2Pac Live (2004)
The Rose, Vol. 2 (2005)
Tupac: Live at the House of Blues (2005) Platinum

Nu-Mixx Klazzics Vol. 2 (2007)
The Early Years (2007)

TOP 10 BILLBOARD SINGLES
"Brenda's Got a Baby" (1991) #3 Rap
"If My Homie Calls" (1991) #3 Rap
"I Get Around" (1993) #8 Rap
"Keep Ya Head Up" (1993) #7 Hip-Hop
"Dear Mama" (1995) #3 Hip-Hop
"Old School" (1995) #1 Rap
"So Many Tears" (1995) #6 Rap
"California Love" (1996) #1 Rap #1 US
"How Do You Want It" (1996) #1 Rap #1 US
"To Live and Die in LA" (1997) #10 US
"Made Niggaz" (1997) #1 Rap
"Do for Love" (1997) #2 Rap
"Changes" (1998) #3 Rap
"Thugz Mansion" (2002) #4 Rap
"Runnin" (2003) #5 Rap
"Ghetto Gospel" (2005) #1 UK
"Pac's Life" (2006) #4 Hip-Hop

FILMOGRAPHY

Nothing but Trouble, Warner Brothers Pictures, 1991.
Played himself.

Juice, Paramount Home Video, 1992. Played Bishop. First
major role.

Poetic Justice, Columbia TriStar Motion Pictures, 1993.
Played Lucky. First starring role.

Above the Rim, New Line Cinema, 1994. Played Birdie.

Bullet, New Line Home Video, 1996. Played Tank. Released
after his death.

Gridlock'd, Gramercy Pictures, 1997. Played Spoon. Released
after his death.

Gang Related, Orion Pictures, 1997. Played Detective Rodri-
guez. His last performance in a film.

Thug Angel—The Life of an Outlaw, QD3 Entertainment, 2002.

Tupac: Resurrection, Amaru Entertainment, MTV Networks,
Viacom, 2003. Documentary.

1947 Alice Fay Williams (she will later change her name to Afeni Shakur) is born in Lumberton, North Carolina.

1971 Tupac Amaru Shakur is born on June 16.

1982 At age 11, Tupac becomes a member of the 127th Street Ensemble.

1984 Tupac moves to Baltimore, Maryland, with his mother and sister, Sekyiwa.

1988 The family moves to Marin City, California.

1990 Tupac tours with the Digital Underground.

1991 Tupac records "Same Song" for Digital Underground's album *This Is an EP Record.* Tupac's debut album

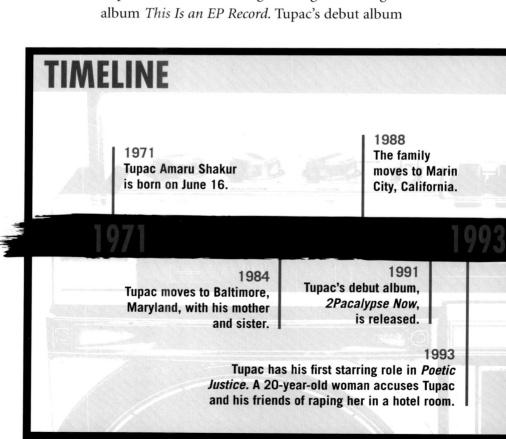

TIMELINE

1971
Tupac Amaru Shakur
is born on June 16.

1988
The family
moves to Marin
City, California.

1971

1993

1984
Tupac moves to Baltimore,
Maryland, with his mother
and sister.

1991
Tupac's debut album,
2Pacalypse Now,
is released.

1993
Tupac has his first starring role in *Poetic
Justice.* A 20-year-old woman accuses Tupac
and his friends of raping her in a hotel room.

with Interscope Records, *2Pacalypse Now,* is released on October 12.

1992   Tupac plays the role of Bishop in *Juice.* In August, a six-year-old boy is shot and killed during fighting at an outdoor Tupac concert.

1993   *Strictly 4 My N.I.G.G.A.Z.* is released in February. Tupac has his first starring role, as Lucky in *Poetic Justice,* opposite Janet Jackson. In November, a 20-year-old woman accuses Tupac and his friends of raping her in a hotel room.

1994   On November 30, Tupac is shot five times while entering a NYC recording studio.

1996
Tupac films movies *Gridlock'd* and *Gang Related.* In February, Tupac's double album, *All Eyez on Me,* is released. September 7, he is shot while riding in a car driven by Suge Knight in Las Vegas. Tupac dies of cardiac arrest and respiratory failure.

1994   1996

1994
Tupac is shot five times while entering a NYC recording studio.

1995
February 7 Tupac is sentenced to prison on sexual assault charges.
September 16 Tupac signs a deal with Suge Knight and Death Row Records.
October 10 He is released from prison after serving 8 months of his sentence.

1995 Tupac is sentenced to prison on sexual assault charges on February 7 and starts his prison term on February 14. In March, *Me Against the World* is released. He marries Keisha Morris on April 29, while in jail, but the marriage is annulled six months later. On September 16, Tupac signs a deal with Suge Knight and Death Row Records. He is released from prison on October 10 after serving eight months of his sentence.

1996 Tupac films movies *Gridlock'd* and *Gang Related,* which are released in 1997. He starts his company, Euphanasia. In February, Tupac's double album, *All Eyez on Me,* is released. On August 27, Tupac leaves Death Row Records. On September 7, he is shot while riding in a car driven by Suge Knight in Las Vegas. On September 13, Tupac dies of cardiac arrest and respiratory failure after he is taken off a life-support system. *The Don Killuminati: The 7 Day Theory* is released that November.

bling Also known as "bling-bling," the symbols of wealth and status such as expensive and rare jewels, cars, money, and clothing. Term may have been coined in 1999 by artist Lil' Wayne, or by the group the Silvertones in "Bling Bling Christmas." Some say the term refers to the "sound" a diamond makes when it sparkles, or similarly, the sound of a gold medallion when it is put on or taken off. Some rappers pursue bling, and some criticize the pursuit of it.

Bloods Los Angeles-based street gang with many chapters around the country. Sworn enemy of the Crips. Bloods wear color red. Allegedly founded in late 1960s by Sylvester Scott and Vincent Owens.

blunts Marijuana cigarettes.

chrome Handgun or a kind of wheel rim on a car.

Crips Thought to stand for "Community Restoration in Progress," a Los Angeles-based gang that may have been formed to help with neighborhood revitalization but soon became a more traditional gang, using and dealing illegal drugs. Sworn enemy of the Bloods. Gang color is navy blue.

deck Turntable.

DJ Short for "disc jockey," the DJ usually mixes rhythmic passes of an album on a turntable or deck.

East Coast One faction of rapping, originated by Public Enemy and the Beastie Boys, and carried on by rapper Biggie Smalls and Sean "Puffy" Combs (later known as P. Diddy), who started Bad Boy Records in 1993 as a college student.

gangsta Variant of the "gangster," a term for organized crime forces. Gangstas tend to be disorganized, urban-based tough guys, often African Americans.

gangsta rap   A form of hip-hop music that seemed to promote violence, promiscuity, and drug use. Generally agreed to have started in the late 1980s.

graffiti   Usually illegal art spray painted on walls, trains, buses, or other public surfaces without permission. Also called graf. The same piece of graffiti can be called art or vandalism, depending on the observer.

hip-hop   A style of music and culture that came to the United States from Jamaica in the 1970s and became a part of mainstream culture in the 1980s. Typically, hip-hop music uses rhyming lyrics accompanied by a drum or other pronounced beat. In addition to a beat, other sounds may be synthesized or performed. Hip-hop culture is usually said to include graffiti art and break dancing. Rap music is a part of the hip-hop culture.

MC   General meaning is master of ceremonies, also spelled "emcee." The coordinating or dominant voice of a hip-hop song or entertainment event. Can also stand for "microphone controller," "music commentator" and much more. The MC usually rhymes to a track of percussive sounds from, or sounding as if from, a drum.

rap   Generally considered the musical component of hip-hop culture. Rap has freestyle music, usually a drum or synthesized beat in the background, and rhymed lyrics.

roadie   A member of the road crew that travels with a band; usually technicians who often ride in sleeper buses.

West Coast   A faction of rapping, originated by N.W.A. and Dr. Dre, and carried on by Snoop Dogg and Tupac Shakur.

BIBLIOGRAPHY

Chambers, Veronica. "Gangsta Life, Gangsta Death." *Esquire,* December 1, 1996. http://www.highbeam.com.

Dyson, Michael Eric. "Tupac: Life Goes On: Why the Rapper Still Appeals to Fans and Captivates Scholars a Decade After His Death." *Black Issues Book Review,* September 1, 2006. http://www.highbeam.com.

Gladwell, Malcolm. "The Rapper's New Rage: Tupac Shakur Had an Epiphany of Sorts." *Washington Post,* December 17, 1993. http://www.highbeam.com.

Hoye, Jacob, and Karolyn Ali, editors. *Tupac: Resurrection.* New York: Atria Books, 2003.

Joseph, Jamal. *Tupac Shakur Legacy.* New York: Atria Books, 2006.

Pinker, Steven. *The Blank Slate.* New York: Viking, 2002.

Scott, Cathy. *The Killing of Tupac Shakur.* Las Vegas: Huntington Press, 2002.

Shakur, Tupac. *The Rose that Grew from Concrete.* New York: Pocket Books, 1999.

▸ ▸▸ FURTHER READING ▪ ▮▮

BOOKS

Dyson, Michael Eric. *Holler if You Hear Me: Searching for Tupac Shakur.* New York: Basic Books, 2001.

Lee, Felicia. "A 'Spiritual Mother' of Spoken Word for a Hip-Hop Generation." *The New York Times,* January 29, 2005. http://selectnytimes.com.

Samuels, Allison. "Rising Up: Tupac Shakur Was Murdered in 1996. In a New Documentary, He Leaps Off the Screen to Tell His Own Story." *Newsweek,* November 24, 2003. http://www.highbeam.com.

Sanneh, Kelefa. "Music: Uneasy Lies the Head." *The New York Times,* November 19, 2006. http://selectnytimes.com.

Sullivan, Randall. *Labyrinth: A Detective Investigates the Murders of Tupac Shakur and Biggie Smalls.* Boston: Atlantic Monthly Press, 2002.

WEB SITES

http://www.2paclegacy.com

http://www.tasf.org

http://www.2paclegacytour.com

PHOTO CREDITS

INDEX

▶ ▸▸ ABOUT THE AUTHORS ■ ‖

CLIFFORD W. MILLS is a writer and editor living in Jacksonville, Florida. He has written biographies of Derek Jeter, Bernie Williams, Curt Schilling, Pope Benedict XVI, and Virginia Woolf. He has compiled a volume of essays about J. D. Salinger, and has been an editor for John Wiley and Sons and Oxford University Press.

CHUCK D redefined rap music and hip-hop culture as leader and cofounder of legendary rap group Public Enemy. His messages addressed weighty issues about race, rage, and inequality with a jolting combination of intelligence and eloquence. A musician, writer, radio host, television guest, college lecturer, and activist, he is the creator of Rapstation.com, a multi-format home on the Web for the vast global Hip Hop community.